MAXIMIZE

YOUR BUSINESS

SUCCESS

-

DON'T OVERLOOK

THE OBVIOUS

PREFACE
(Or, Who Is This 'Russell A. Irving'?)

Years ago, someone asked me whether I was a Modern-day Renaissance Man or someone who could not hold down a job. This was a reasonable question to ask, as over the decades, I have held a fair number of positions, in a number of professional fields.

What is known as 'the Private Sector' became 'my home' for years. I was a general manager for a chain of family restaurants. I owned a retail technology business. And...

Much time was spent in what is known as Human Services. I worked with a wide assortment of individuals who had differing struggles to overcome.
I was: a counselor, group home manager, residential treatment center coordinator, health and sexuality advisor, workshop manager, and therapeutic group leader, among other positions.

Government work with city and state entities has played a large role in my work experiences. I was primarily involved with: Job Training programs and Risk Management matters.
My specialties included: Staff Training, Software Development, Program Evaluation & Auditing, Liason Work, and Management.

I created and conducted numerous classes/workshops covering a wide array of topics: Single Life, Time Management, Marriage Enrichment, and Entrepreneurship, among them.

Writing has been a strong passion of mine.
I wrote for and published a unique, tasteful magazine geared toward single adults. Had a stint as a columnist for a special interest newspaper, as well as one for an online news site. I frequently blog. And, became the author of several books.
Which almost takes me (finally) to **Maximize Your Business**

Success - Don't Overlook The Obvious.

In 2008, after becoming fed-up watching 'experts' claim that there was a 'magic bullet' to relationship success, I decided that '*Enough was enough!*'.

Over the decades I had learned: #1 That there was no one, simple *or* complicated solution to any of life's issues, including relationship ones. #2 That people were turned off by psychobabble. #3 That we live in a 'Headline News' and 'Twitter' society where folks want bottom-line info.

The key to solving most issues and getting what one wants lay in 'The Obvious'. - Advice that most people ignored because it appeared to be trite, or steps that they did not wish to take.

So, I wrote ***Improve Your Marriage - Don't Overlook The Obvious***, which contained over 500 pieces of advice/tips. No chapters, because life does not happen that way. No psychobbale. Advice in an average of only 1-3 sentences.

Response to the book was great! I have had dozens of radio/talk show interviews based upon it! Around the country!

Which led me write, ***Teens! Improve Your Life - Don't Overlook The Obvious***. - A similarly formatted book containing hundreds of life skill advice for teens. The response has also been wonderful!

*Now, after business owners have asked me to do another in the **'Don't Overlook The Obvious'** series, comes this volume. Geared toward business managrs and owners. (Much of it also suitable for those in the non-profit and government sectors.)*

I wish success to those of you willing to follow at least some of the 500+ suggestions to be found here. - Hopefully, you will share the book with others. - And, perhaps there will be a time when you will send me at Russ@MaximizeYourBusinessSuccess.com, your own tales of success resulting from trying some of what I present for your consideration and action.

So, without further ado...

INTRODUCTION

Whether you are a business owner, executive, or manager, your work life is simultaneously: Exciting, yet mundane. Financially profitable and draining of resources. Stable, yet always on the verge of achieving new heights or falling off of a cliff into the depths of a ravine. Where days pass all too quickly, or seem to never end. A source of new relationships and a wedge between existing and dear-to-your-heart ones. Where tried and true principles still can exist, while new ones challenge you to keep up.

Businesses fail with great frequency, The economy rises and falls, with the heaving of the stock exchanges and monetary ruling bodies.
Schools churn out countless young women and men, all hoping to be the next Warren Buffet, Martha Stewart, Elon Musk, Oprah Winfrey, Sir Richard Branson, or Martha Lane Fox. Yet, so many of these hopefuls are employed as waitresses, stock boys, or entry-level assistant managers at the local fast food emporium.
Society pages speak of longterm marriages on-the-rocks or which have already plummeted to their death.
Embezzlers, swindlers, and con artists appear on wanted posters, on *American Greed*, and in your PC's emails.
Vacations tend to involve smartphones bulging from swim trunks, tennis shorts, and purses.
Family time tends to revolve around *any* spare moment when you can actually 'get away from it all'.

Technology has transformed many a business, while some languish by the roadside, along with other vestiges of a time gone by.

24-hour news cycles hawk exclusives with the latest scandals' victims. Social media exposes our daily quirks. Minutiae which used to be our own business now belongs to 'The Public-At-Large'.

What do we do about this?
What can *you* do about this?

Maximize Your Business Success – Don't Overlook the Obvious
is a part of the answer.
* *It is a guide,* if you will, with brief strategies, truisms, and ideas,
  which when turned into action, should help your business and
  professional life to grow.
* *It should help novice as well as seasoned executives and
  entrepreneurs* to reach new heights of success.
* *It should be 'must reading'* for business, trade, and law school
  students, among others, who want a leg up when they find
  themselves smack in the middle of 'The Workplace'.
* *It should help to free-up time and energy* so that friends and
  family, as well as 'alone time', get their fair share of you.

There are no chapters. Because every day brings new issues with
which to contend. And they seldom arrive in any specific order or
even with the same amount of importance

Read the book in stages. Not all at once. Then, go back to it, again
and again. *You will be amazed* at how something will strike a
chord, when it did not, previously, because it wasn't the right time.

Repetition is the key to learning almost anything (as any teacher
knows), as well as a key to changing behaviors. (Which is why we
remember and often act upon frequently aired advertisements).
Also, people respond better to some phrases than they do to others.
Therefore, I have repeated some messages, with different wording.

"That's obvious." or "Trite." - These are expected comments to
some of the pages' contents.
But, we tend to overlook 'The Obvious' in our daily life. We tend to
make problems overly complex and difficult to solve. We forget
that simply expressed ideas are so often, ultimately, the most vital.

Haven't you read about or even experienced a situation where you think, "How could they have let such a simple matter result in the business crumbling, give way to new competitors, or fail due to not heeding the most basic of concepts?"

It's often '*The Obvious*' solution that is going to provide the best results. (Not necessarily the simplest one to implement, but the *best* option, when all is said and done.)

Maximize Your Business Success – Don't Overlook the Obvious aims to 'bottom-line' common and not-so-common-sense rules and tips for a successful career and, for some of you, a wildly prosperous business!

No one size fits all, in shoes, or in the workplace.
There is no 'magic bullet' or single 'key to success', so not everything will apply to all readers. -- You should instinctively know what makes sense for your particular situation, when you read it. -- And, because life, work, and needs change, what applies today might not tomorrow, and so on. Thus, making this a perfect 'ongoing' reference book.

So, while what is suggested will work well for many people, there is always the possibility that it *might* not work well for you.
Therefore, do not blindly follow what is offered here.
This book is not intended as a substitute for those of you who need 'heavy-duty' consulting assistance.
Use common sense. Think about how these steps and ideas might fit into your specific circumstances.
Then, make your own decisions and take responsibility for them.

Do your best! That is truly, all that one can ever do. And, what your business/employer deserves!

Now, go take that step toward (further) success! You deserve it!
Wishing you the best that life has to offer,

Russell A. Irving

**Practice LEAN
In management,
Production, and sales.**

~~~~~~~~~~~

**Customers are not
Always correct.
So, don't always act
As though they are.**

~~~~~~~~~~~

**A fear of compromise
Is a fear of the loss
Of your control.**
Get over that fear, to succeed!

~~~~~~~~~~~

**Develop your 'Brand'.
It matters.**

**If you haven't
Screwed-up lately,
You've been complacent.**

~~~~~~~~~

**Some clients
Will always complain.
*So what?***

~~~~~~~~~~

**You don't accept excuses
From your managers and
Other employees.
So why do you believe that
They want to hear *yours*?**

~~~~~~~~~~

**Clutter is less 'Genius'
And more 'Mess'.**

Social media can
Close doors to additional business,
As easily as it can open them.
So, proceed with caution.

~~~~~~~~~~

Growing your business
Too quickly
Can be as disastrous
As being stagnant.

~~~~~~~~~~

Lighting, flooring, ergonomics,
And air quality,
All have a very real impact
On employees/clients/customers.

~~~~~~~~~~

Loyalty breeds loyalty.

Mine your data.
If you don't know how,
Then find someone who does.
Data *'rules' and generates profits.*

~~~~~~~~~~~~

Develop a *Business Continuity Plan.*

~~~~~~~~~~~~

Foolish companies
Do not foster employee loyalty.
Wise ones that do so
Will survive many a crisis.

~~~~~~~~~~~~

Your body language
Is often believed
More than your words.

Crap happens.
Expect it.
Try to plan for it.
Knowing that it's not always possible.

~~~~~~~~~~~

Form bonds with co-workers,
But make them professional ones.

~~~~~~~~~~~

The odds are only 50/50
That your children will want
To run your company.
So plan accordingly

~~~~~~~~~~~

Recognize when it's the time
To lay-off or fire
Line staff or management.

How many 'shortcuts'
Have taken you longer
Than the path that
You chose to avoid?

~~~~~~~~~~~

Unless you know *all* of
Your business' operating costs,
How could you possibly price
Your product or service?

~~~~~~~~~~~

Never pay only the minimum wage.
Even if the wage that you give
Is only a quarter higher.
(*Perception is reality.*)

~~~~~~~~~~~

Use '*mystery shoppers*'.

**Don't be crude.
Even if you think that customers
Or staff cannot hear you,
Or that they wouldn't mind.**

~~~~~~~~~~~

Have a written, detailed dress code.

~~~~~~~~~~~

**The manner in which
You layoff staff
Will set the tone
For those employees
Who remain.**

~~~~~~~~~~~

**Speak critically of competitors
In a *'generic manner'*.**

Realize that people
Will not always understand
Your point of view.
Let alone, agree with it.
That's okay.

~~~~~~~~~~

Be very judicious
When telling management or staff
"Because I say so." or
"Because I am the boss."

~~~~~~~~~~

Policies for dealing with robberies
Should be clear
And reviewed at least semi-annually.

~~~~~~~~~~

Do not over-automate.

Practice.
What?
Your weakest
And **your strongest areas.**

~~~~~~~~~~~

Deliver meeting agendas
At least 1 business day ahead of time.

~~~~~~~~~~~

How much would it cost
To stock your waiting room
With current magazines?
(*Hint*: Less than you would think.
Appreciated more than you imagine!)

~~~~~~~~~~~

Accuracy counts.
Take your time.

Government contracts
While potentially very lucrative
Come with an incredible
Amount of red tape.

~~~~~~~~~~~

Fight the common urge of making
Financial commitments
Based upon
Overly optimistic projections.

~~~~~~~~~~~

If you offer coupons,
Don't allow those without one
To get the special deal.
Otherwise, resentment builds among
Those who followed your rules.
(And *they* are your best customers.)

~~~~~~~~~~~

Sometimes,
Getting deserved credit
For work well done
Will cost you more
Than you will gain.

~~~~~~~

If company policy allows it,
Have your own style
In the way that you dress.

~~~~~~~

Active shooter training,
For large *or* small firms
Could possibly save lives.

~~~~~~~

Do not create
Fake testimonials.

Wise competitors will
Check out your business.
Prepare to do the same.

~~~~~~~~~~~~

There is a difference
Between '*Negativity*' and
'*Critical Evaluation*'.

~~~~~~~~~~~~

Some employees
Will never '*play well, together*'.
Recognize who they are
And deal with them.

~~~~~~~~~~~~

Monitor the cost of supplies
(Both office and cleaning),
Or you could bust your budgets.

Know what these mean:
TOR
VPN
Hack
Breach
Spear Phishing
Zero-Day Flaw.

~~~~~~~~~

Allow employees
To respond to evaluations.

~~~~~~~~~

Self-promotion
Is a vital component
Of being successful.

~~~~~~~~~

Donate to local charities.

**Clearly post
Clear & concise
'Return Policies'.**

~~~~~~~~~~

**Be friendly with
Employees, bosses, and customers.
But don't be their *close* friend.**

~~~~~~~~~~

**Create opportunities
For *'leadership education'*
And experience.**

~~~~~~~~~~

**Badmouthing of your company
Is unacceptable,
Regardless of which employee does it.**

Always know which lawyer
You would go to, as needed.
Lawyers are not experts in
All areas.

~~~~~~~~~

Not everyone has the funds
With which to join others
For after-hours drinks or...
Be sensitive to that fact.

~~~~~~~~~

Save $
By buying in bulk,
But *only if* an analysis
Proves it to be cost-effective.

~~~~~~~~~

Reward innovation.

Be suspicious of others
Who offer to let you
Take credit for their work.

~~~~~~~~~~

Seek out media coverage.
Free publicity is awesome!

~~~~~~~~~~

There are many reasons to
Pay staff on a weekly basis.

~~~~~~~~~~

It's wiser to admit
Not knowing something
And saying that you will
Seek out the information,
Then it is to bluff or lie
And getting caught doing it.

How likely is it that
You will regret not having
An updated resume, on hand?

~~~~~~~~~~

If you are an unpaid intern,
Know what the legal parameters are.
Do not let the company
Take advantage of you.

~~~~~~~~~~

Hold periodic focus groups,
But only if you know how to run one.
Otherwise, hire someone
Who does know how.

~~~~~~~~~~

Utilize job training programs
To hire, train, and retain staff.

Allowing workers smoking breaks,
In addition to their standard ones,
Will result in animosity from others.

~~~~~~~~~~

Personal mobile devices
Should not house PII
(*Personally Identifiable Information*)

~~~~~~~~~~

Pay attention to research.

~~~~~~~~~~

Employee theft
Will drive up costs,
Thus driving away profits.
So, root it out!
Now.

Schedule your sales staff
Based upon historical data,
Not upon the number of widgets
That you have available.
(Or some other arbitrary,
Illogical method.)

~~~~~~~~~~

Smart retail or food managers *'float'*
And do not *'tread water'*,
By staying in the same spot
(*e.g.*, the office).

~~~~~~~~~~

Snarky comments
Will eventually cause you Losses.
Were they worth it?

~~~~~~~~~~

Stress will kill.
Sleep, relaxing activities, exercise,
And time with family and friends
Can help to save you, them,
And your business.

~~~~~~~~~~~

Co-Op advertising
Is often overlooked,
Yet it is often valuable.

~~~~~~~~~~~

Give the references that you receive,
Limited credibility and weight.
Go more by
Your gut and investigation.

~~~~~~~~~~~

Know when to turn off technology.

Giving in to the customer
Who throws a temper tantrum/scene
Sets a bad precedence for others
And hurts employee morale.

~~~~~~~~~~

How have you planned for
The potential splitting up
Of your partnership agreement?

~~~~~~~~~~

There is often staff '*fallout*'
When you transfer someone
Out of a location.

~~~~~~~~~~

Take your doctors' warnings
Seriously.
Unlike too many of your peers.

The real problem
Is not asking for help
When you need it.
So hang your ego up
In your closet.

~~~~~~~~~~

Pets in the workplace
Can reduce stress
And increase productivity.
(*In the proper setting.*)

~~~~~~~~~~

If you always do the honorable thing,
You won't need to keep looking
Over your shoulder.

~~~~~~~~~~

Update your resume, quarterly.

Not responding to
Emails, voicemail, or letters,
Is often taken as
A personal affront.

~~~~~~~~~~~~

Don't be annoyed or show it
When an employee or customer
Asks you a question.
Even that '*really stupid one*'.

~~~~~~~~~~~~

Learn your company's culture.
(Not only that of your own unit.)

~~~~~~~~~~~~

Pay heed to
What your office's decor
Says about you.

Be prepared to follow through
With consequences for bad
Employee behavior.
Or else *you*
Will '*face the consequences*'!

~~~~~~~~~~

'Working harder' succeeds
With great results
When coupled with
'Working smarter'.

~~~~~~~~~~

Consider
Giving *unexpected* bonuses
When business is great.

~~~~~~~~~~

Diversify your media buys.

Remember to accommodate
Disabled employees and customers.
Because it is the 'right thing to do'
And, because it is the law.

~~~~~~~~~~

Gossip is not limited
To the water-cooler.
Try to flush any of it
'Down the drain',
Before it damages
Too many people and your goals.

~~~~~~~~~~

Brainstorm
Potential problems
And potential solutions.
Don't rely only on your own ideas.

~~~~~~~~~~

What motivates a specific employee,
Will change over the course of time.
Stay in touch with what that is
At every point in time.

~~~~~~~~~~

Don't allow employees
To intimidate or boss you around.
No exceptions.

~~~~~~~~~~

Don't allow list-making
To prevent you
From being productive.

~~~~~~~~~~

Don't be offensive,
If only to avoid being
'Politically incorrect'.

Ignoring or sloughing off criticism
Is a recipe for failure.
Instead, evaluate it,
As objectively as you can.

~~~~~~~~~

Study after study shows that
Naps increase productivity
In many/most individuals.

~~~~~~~~~

'Book knowledge'
And *'Street Smarts'*
Go hand-in-hand.

~~~~~~~~~

Don't try to impress others
By using industry lingo
Unless you know what it means.

Avoid being the person
Who doesn't let facts
'*Get in their way*'.

~~~~~~~~~~

Trust should be,
Yet too often isn't,
A 2-way street.

~~~~~~~~~~

Don't steal from work.
Anything.
Period.

~~~~~~~~~~

Don't hire trainers
Sight unseen.

~~~~~~~~~~

Your '*Community*'
Includes more than
Your immediate geographic area.
Think '*Internet*' or
'*Special Population*'.

~~~~~~~~~~

Take in business partners
With great trepidation,
Hesitation,
And great legal advice.

~~~~~~~~~~

The silliest or 'off-the-wall' ideas
Can lead to profitable results.
So, give them serious consideration.

~~~~~~~~~~

Don't waste a customer's time.

Success often takes place
On the front-line level.
Not in the executive suite.

~~~~~~~~~~

Be prepared for failure.
Just don't anticipate it.
Otherwise, you are inviting it in.

~~~~~~~~~~

Maintain proper
Employee records.

~~~~~~~~~~

Unfortunately, a few of you
Might need the following advice
And take it to heart:
Avoid discrimination.

Better to '*under*'
Than '*over*' promise.

~~~~~~~~~~

Support by family
And significant others
Will impact your business's
Success, job satisfaction, or both.

~~~~~~~~~~

Your appearance matters.
To customers, clients, staff,
Creditors, vendors...
Most everyone!

~~~~~~~~~~

An open-door policy
Without *any* restrictions
Is corporate suicide.

Why do you believe that
Your business must grow
In order to be considered
A success?

~~~~~~~~~~

Customers are not always '*right*'.
Yet, you do not need
To '*publicize*' that fact.

~~~~~~~~~~

Respect your customer's culture.
But, you don't have to embrace it.

~~~~~~~~~~

Consider subsidizing
The cost of employees' uniforms,
If you do not supply them.

'Helicopter Bosses'
Eventually go into a tail-spin,
Crashing & burning.
With numerous casualties.

~~~~~~~~~~

Review and update job descriptions
On a regular schedule.

~~~~~~~~~~

Discipline or fire staff
In person.
Not by email, telephone,
Mail, or other impersonal means.

~~~~~~~~~~

Don't tell customers "*Because...* "
In response to their questions.

Get advice regarding
Wage and hour policies
From experts.
And review them,
At least, annually.

~~~~~~~~~~

When possible,
Provide generous severance packages.

~~~~~~~~~~

Do you know how badly
That you need this job?
Unless you do,
Your decisions are apt
To be flawed, to some extent.

~~~~~~~~~~

Have several trusted advisors.

Know whom your employees
Truly trust and listen to.
Then enlist that person
To help you achieve your goals.

~~~~~~~~~~

Not all franchises will succeed.
Perform due diligence
Before investing in one.

~~~~~~~~~~

Be open to suggestions,
But don't become overwhelmed.

~~~~~~~~~~

Any bluffing or lying
By *any* employee or board member
Will become apparent.
(Not '*if*', but '*when*'.)

Do not display a suggestion box
And never implement *any* ideas
That staff submit.

~~~~~~~~~~

Pay employees
What they are worth
Or the industry standard,
Whichever is greater,
(*If you can afford to do it,*
Whether or not you want to do so.)

~~~~~~~~~~

Take advantage of
College internships.
But follow tax and employment regs.

~~~~~~~~~~

Always file your taxes on time.

Family owned/operated businesses
Are a *'different animal'*.
They need to be tamed
To avoid bitter fighting
By their *'various inhabitants'*.

~~~~~~~~~

Everyone has a reputation at work.
Make yours a great one.

~~~~~~~~~

Do you really require an office?
Or, will a desk do, as well?
(In other words, shouldn't you spend
Most of your time as a manager
'Where the action is'?)

~~~~~~~~~

Reward loyalty.

Assist laid-off workers
With their job search efforts.
It's the '*right thing*' to do
And builds great '*credit*'
With the remaining employees.

~~~~~~~~~~

Gross income
Is less important than
Net profit.

~~~~~~~~~~

Be leery, at least initially,
Of the employee
Who applied for your job,
Did not get it,
And yet stayed on with the company.

~~~~~~~~~~

Be careful when you create
Your social media/email username.
Be professional.

~~~~~~~~~~~~

Be careful:
Joint ventures can backfire
If the other company's reputation
Is less than stellar.
So, do your '*homework*'
Before committing.

~~~~~~~~~~~~

Customers and employees
Do not want to watch you
Chew gum or tobacco.

~~~~~~~~~~~~

Try to be flexible with scheduling.

Having a workplace violence policy
Should not be an option in this age.

~~~~~~~~~~~~

What if your key vendors
Go out of business?
Do you know how to
Get a fast replacement for them?

~~~~~~~~~~~~

Pay attention to
Customer complaints
Even if you don't agree
That they are valid.
(This does not mean, however,
That you should
Always give in to the customer.)

~~~~~~~~~~~~

Assume that your systems
Will be breached, someday.
Plan for your company's reactions,
Including legal obligations.
(*Especially*, as not all government
Entities have the same requirements.)

~~~~~~~~~~

'*Faking it*'
Might bring you transient success,
But usually yields enduring failure.

~~~~~~~~~~

Don't confuse
Questioning authority
With being defiant.
They can be quite different.

~~~~~~~~~~

Innovation,
No matter how logical,
Will not always be welcomed.
(By clients, employees, or...)
So, tread carefully.

~~~~~~~~~~

Don't create awards
To give yourself or your business.
People will discover this,
And it will backfire.

~~~~~~~~~~

Enforce a ban on the
Hazing of employees.

~~~~~~~~~~

Surround yourself
With talent and earned loyalty.

Your tolerance for risk
Is crucial information
Before you decide upon
A new job or starting a business.

~~~~~~~~~~

There are benefits to
Fading into the background.
But they come with the risk
That you would also become
The most expendable person
When layoffs occur.

~~~~~~~~~~

Decide whether the number of hours
An employee spends
At the office, store, or plant
Matters more than their productivity.

~~~~~~~~~~

Groom others
To assume key positions
In the event of
Unexpected illness or death.

~~~~~~~~~~

Time is both
Your '*Enemy*'
And your '*Friend*'.
Decide which one it usually is.
If the former, invest in
'*Time management*' training.

~~~~~~~~~~

You can and should always work on
Your positive attitude.
(It matters.)

~~~~~~~~~~

You likely never know
'*Who*' is listening
Or who in your audience
Is related to '*Whom*'.
But there is power in knowing it.

~~~~~~~~~

Sometimes it is wise
To break-up with
A long-time employee,
Just as it can be
To break-up with
A spouse.

~~~~~~~~~

Be positive
When negatively portraying
Your competitors.

~~~~~~~~~

Learn who has the *actual*
Decision-making power.
It might surprise you.

~~~~~~~~~~

Don't choose your business site
Based upon a '*gut feeling*'
Or because your significant other
Is enamored of it.

~~~~~~~~~~

Give new ideas sufficient time
To work or fail.
Few things succeed overnight.

~~~~~~~~~~

'*Power naps*' are
A tool of the '*Successful*'.
For a valid reason.

Modify your personal lifestyle
In order to pay down/off your debts.
Because that can result in
Less stress in your work-life.

~~~~~~~~

'*Bait and switch*' tactics
(By any other name)
Will hurt your sales
In the long-run.

~~~~~~~~

Sometimes there is such a
Toxic work environment
That you need to hire
All new staff.

~~~~~~~~

Become tech savvy, if you can.

Avoid looking exhausted,
Especially if you are in
Sales or service.

~~~~~~~~~~

Have access to a
Professional who understands
HIPAA.

~~~~~~~~~~

Wanting to stand out
In the way that you dress
Does not mean that you must
Wear '*gaudy*'.

~~~~~~~~~~

Your off-shoring of jobs
Will have hidden costs.

You can be
The most talented and qualified,
Person in the company.
But if others do not like you,
You could find yourself
Out the door or powerless.

~~~~~~~~~

Whom you trust with your life
Might not be the person
To trust with a business deal.

~~~~~~~~~

Know what the
Americans with Disabilities Act
Expects of you
As an employer and business owner.
Or, face the wrath of
Millions of (*potential*) clients
And '*The Law*'.

Community involvement
Is vital for your success.

~~~~~~~~~~

Know your employees'
Strengths, weaknesses,
And personalities,
Before you get caught off-guard
By your competitors.

~~~~~~~~~~

Changing your job?
Then exit gracefully
And professionally.
Do not '*burn bridges*'.

~~~~~~~~~~

Most people exaggerate
Somewhere on their resume.

Every job
Has it's drawbacks.
Every job.
Just know the limit
Of what you will tolerate
Without diminishing
Your value to the company
Or your family, friends, and health.

~~~~~~~~~~

Different people
Will remember
The same situation,
Differently.
Without any intention
Of lying or misleading.

~~~~~~~~~~

Surround yourself
With brilliance.

Why shouldn't a professional
Or skilled laborer
Bill by the job
And not by the hour?
The former method
Might just be the key
To landing a lucrative job
And gaining a unique reputation.

~~~~~~~~~~~~

Insist on a
'*Foul language-free*' workspace.

~~~~~~~~~~~~

Hoping that you
Will never become
Incapacitated
Or otherwise
Need time away,
Is a recipe for disaster.

Hire a *Risk Manager*,
If only on a consultancy basis.
You can save on countless
And expensive claims
Down the road.

~~~~~~~~~~

Working
And working towards a goal
Are often different matters.
But that should not be the case.

~~~~~~~~~~

Your personal taste
In decor
Matters less
Than what is apt
To appeal to your clientele.

~~~~~~~~~~

Avoiding problems,
Can lead to
Huge catastrophes.
So, don't hide.
Face them head-on.

~~~~~~~~~~

Only trust training
Of new staff
To those who *can* train.
That is not going to be
Your most productive employee
In many instances.
(The old, yet often true adage:
Those who cannot do, teach.)

~~~~~~~~~~

Cybersecurity
Should be high
On every business's priority list.

Allow your verbal agreements
To be binding
Even if they are not legally, so.

~~~~~~~~~

Sighing
When asked a question
Is insulting and can
Cost you a sale or a client.

~~~~~~~~~

Belittling staff,
Yelling at them,
And micromanaging them
Does not make you
An effective leader.
Simply the opposite.

~~~~~~~~~

It's easy to be critical
When you have not experienced
What your employee or client has.

~~~~~~~~~~

Customers do not always
Want to spend their money
At the business
With the nicest ambiance.
Know your customers' preferences.

~~~~~~~~~~

Like it or not,
We live in a multi-lingual country.
Maintain employees
Who can communicate
In commonly spoken languages.

~~~~~~~~~~

Do not tolerate
Clients who mistreat
Your employees.
Otherwise, you will lose
Respect from those
You count on
To make you money.

~~~~~~~~~~

Never date
Or have an affair
With an employee.

~~~~~~~~~~

Invest
In a proper security system.
Or don't complain
When you suffer
An inevitable loss.

Consider the benefits
Of bartering.
As well as it's legal
And tax ramifications.

~~~~~~~~~~~

Return telephone calls.
Reply to emails.
Keep appointments.
In other words,
Do what you want others
To do for you.

~~~~~~~~~~~

There is always
Someone smarter
And more capable than you.
So what?
Keep being your best
At what you do.

Being chronically late
Is an insult,
A theft of payroll,
And a loss of productivity.

~~~~~~~~~

However,
Being the last person
To leave the office,
Habitually,
Does not make you
The most valuable employee.

~~~~~~~~~

Always end a meeting with
Specific action steps.

~~~~~~~~~

Try to promote from within.

Anyone
Who feels entitled
To break the rules,
Should feel obligated
To face the consequences.
Period.

~~~~~~~~~~

Even technically invalid criticism
Is important and needs attention.

~~~~~~~~~~

A source of great
LEAN expertise
· Can be yours
By utilizing interns
From your local university.

~~~~~~~~~~

Your company can be
On the 'cutting edge'
Without involving
The latest, costly technology.
(Think about it!)

~~~~~~~~~~

Oftentimes,
A face-to-face meeting
Is needed
To close the best deal, possible.

~~~~~~~~~~

No one should be
(Considered)
'Irreplaceable'.
Because no one is.
Not even the Boss.

~~~~~~~~~~

Make friends
With your local banker.
You each have a vested interest
In seeing that
The other one succeeds.

~~~~~~~~~~

Personal lives
Do impact the work of
Everyone in the company.
So, be aware of anyone's
Major, life events:
Weddings, births, deaths,
Separations, divorces,
Health crisis, adoptions…

~~~~~~~~~~

Great salespeople
Are not demeaning,
Even when tempted to be.

Avoid looking like a deer
Caught in a headlight,
When upheaval occurs.
Plan. Plan.
And then, plan some more.

~~~~~~~~

Know what your business
Should do if and when
A natural disaster strikes.
Your reaction to a hurricane,
Snowstorm, tornado, flood,
Or earthquake
Will often call for
A different response.

~~~~~~~~

Sometimes,
You have to cut your losses
And consolidate.

Never make nightly bank deposits
At the same time
And without someone else
Following you, in a separate vehicle.

~~~~~~~~~~~~

Don't hold meetings
Simply because
It is the '*1ˢᵗ Thursday of the month*'.
People rightfully so,
Resent a waste of their time.

~~~~~~~~~~~~

Be respectful
Of your employees'
Religious beliefs
And customs.
Just as you expect them
To be respectful of yours.

**Pollsters
Often get it wrong.
Because people
Often wish to keep
Their *true* opinions & beliefs
To themselves.**

~~~~~~~~~~

**Peer pressure
Is not only
A *'Teenage Thing'*.
Be aware of it
And use it to your advantage.**

~~~~~~~~~~

Don't be surprised by corruption.

~~~~~~~~~~

Plans do not have to be complex.

Many of the principles behind
A great personal relationship
Apply to having
A great work relationship.

~~~~~~~~~

If giving employees a cash raise
Is not possible or wise,
Then negotiate for them
To receive *other perks*
That are of value to them.
(The emphasis is on
The previous 8 words.)

~~~~~~~~~

Sincerity can trump
Knowledge.
Yet, only occasionally.

~~~~~~~~~

Not all publicity
Is good for the company,
Contrary to popular belief.

~~~~~~~~~

Lay off employees
In a dignified manner.

~~~~~~~~~

If your business
Would truly *'fall apart'*
Were you to go away on vacation,
Then you have the wrong staff
Or they are trained incorrectly,
If trained, at all.

~~~~~~~~~

Carry extra/external batteries
For your mobile devices.

Offer customers simple amenities.
Many would cost very little,
While building tremendous good will.

~~~~~~~~~~

Do nice things for someone
Before you need or want
To ask them for a favor.

~~~~~~~~~~

If you did something wrong,
The fact that you '*got away with it*'
For now,
Does *not* mean that you *will*
Be able to do so, again,
Or that you will never be caught.

~~~~~~~~~~

Make *your word* mean something.

Do not dangle promotions or raises
Unless you truly intend to
Follow-through with them.
Because if you give them
To someone else,
Be prepared for scorn & sabotage.

~~~~~~~~~~

Someone will overhear you,
Probably when you
Least want them to do so.

~~~~~~~~~~

Telework is not suitable
For every position
Or for every person.

~~~~~~~~~~

Plan for being misunderstood.

Do not tolerate verbal abuse.
Even from customers.

~~~~~~~~~~

Mobile apps
Should be easily read
Even by those
With visual impairments.

~~~~~~~~~~

Don't implement
The latest management fad
Simply to be
A *'cutting edge'* firm.

~~~~~~~~~~

Body language
Does not always mean
What you believe it to mean.

Some competitors
Are not ethical.
And not above spreading lies.
So, keep your eyes and ears
To the ground.

~~~~~~~~~~

Have key lawyers on retainer
Or on the payroll.

~~~~~~~~~~

Burned-out executives
Contribute less and less
To the company's
Growth and profitability.
So. help them to recharge
Or find replacements for them.

~~~~~~~~~~

Have well-defined,
Easily understood,
Social media/computer/
Cell phone policies.

~~~~~~~~~~

Language
Not only matters,
But it needs to be understood
From the vantage point of
Both the speaker and the listener.

~~~~~~~~~~

Know, not guess,
What state, federal, and local
Labor laws are in effect,
Which apply to your business.
Or have someone who does know
At your disposal.

Opinions are not facts.
Know the facts before
You negotiate
With unions, politicians,
Or potential merger suitors.

~~~~~~~~~~

Don't let clients
Know how badly
That you need their business.

~~~~~~~~~~

Make even the maintenance crew
Feel as special
As they truly are.
And, they *are* all special.

~~~~~~~~~~

Save all business receipts.

Pay reasonable
Travel, food, and lodging expenses
For those who go business trips.

~~~~~~~~~~

Think twice before
Supplying alcohol
At business functions,
Thus exposing the firm
And yourself to potential lawsuits.

~~~~~~~~~~

Recognize the signs
Of addiction regarding:
Gambling. Drugs. Alcohol.
Assist affected employees
Get the help that they need.
For the sake of the employee
And the business.

If your customer base
Skews toward the senior citizen
As opposed to 'everyone',
Then you need to begin
Reaching out to a younger set.
Now!

~~~~~~~~~~

Choose board members carefully.
Because their baggage
Will become your baggage.

~~~~~~~~~~

Sharing anecdotes
When leading a presentation
With '*dry material*'
Will help you to
Keep participants' attention.

~~~~~~~~~~

How can you avoid
Having to deal
With whistleblowers?
Simple!
Run a *'clean'* operation
Through and through.
And listen to those
Who want to tell you of problems
So that they get dealt with, internally.

~~~~~~~~~~

Be able to spot
The difference between
Your gut feeling
And what you logically
Know should be done.

~~~~~~~~~~

Investigate the potential benefits
Of leasing space and equipment.

Listen to your staff's opinions.
But, ultimately,
You are the '*boss*'.
You must make
And own the decision.

~~~~~~~~~

People tend to resent ads
That put-down their competitors,
Instead of explaining why
Their business is the best.

~~~~~~~~~

Request.
Don't demand
A raise.

~~~~~~~~~

Anything is theoretically negotiable.

Learn the differences among:
Virus
Malware
Spyware.

~~~~~~~~~~

**Know when to '*dress the part*'
and when not to.**

~~~~~~~~~~

**Just as dogs don't eat or sleep
Where they s__t,
Avoid indulging in
Workplace romance.**

~~~~~~~~~~

Buy '*Local*' whenever possible.

~~~~~~~~~~

Learn about your competitors.
What you can easily see
On the '*surface*'
And what '*lies below*'.

~~~~~~~~~~

Turn down business
If you have serious, realistic doubts
About succeeding.

~~~~~~~~~~

High sales volume
Does not necessarily equal
High profits.

~~~~~~~~~~

Utilize the many
Free and valuable
Mobile apps.

Avoid whispering.
It breeds rumors, fear,
Paranoia, and anger.

~~~~~~~~~~

When upgrading technology,
Offer your surplus items to
Small, under-funded, non-profits.
They are often the least able
To afford the equipment
That they need.

~~~~~~~~~~

The adage:
"Take your fight outside."
Applies to management, as well.
Don't argue in front of clients or staff.

~~~~~~~~~~

When you decide to celebrate
Only certain holidays
With a day off for employees,
You will likely offend others.
Be prepared to respond with
A caring attitude and a justification.
Or, better yet, respond by offering
Time off to those other employees.

~~~~~~~~~

Write things down.
Memories are fallible.

~~~~~~~~~

'*Arguing*' is not the same
As '*Disagreeing*' or '*Asserting*'
Your rights or points of view.

~~~~~~~~~

Continuous improvement
Is not always a realistic goal
For the short term.
But, it must remain
A critical, long-term goal.

~~~~~~~~~~

The size and furnishings
Of your office
Tell others what you are like,
Whether or not that view is accurate.

~~~~~~~~~~

Do not be afraid of compromising.
It's often the best route to success.

~~~~~~~~~~

Do not let them know
How badly you need this job.

Don't tolerate 'set-ups'
Whether created
By your staff or bosses.

~~~~~~~~~~

Know that '*drama*',
Even if it is not exaggerated,
Can be viewed as unbelievable.

~~~~~~~~~~

If you are frustrated,
Do something about it.
Don't be complacent.

~~~~~~~~~~

Multitasking has been shown
To make you less effective.
Not more.

Pay attention to
Current stories in the news.
Somewhere lurking in 1/more of them
Is likely something that can impact
Your business strategy.

~~~~~~~~~~

Know the vernacular
Used in your trade.
Both the '*formal*'
And '*informal*' ones.

~~~~~~~~~~

Ethnic slurs
Should not be tolerated.
Period.

~~~~~~~~~~

Hire tax professionals.

Asthmatics & the chemically sensitive
Should be considered
When re-decorating workspaces.

~~~~~~~~~~

Bosses should be impressed
By '*effort*' as well as by '*success*'.
Although they should not be
Equally compensated.

~~~~~~~~~~

A *seemingly* defiant action
Could save your company $
Or enhance it's image.
So, separate your emotional reaction
From an objective analysis,
Before taking negative action
Against the employee involved.

~~~~~~~~~~

The best locations often fail
Due to a lack of strategic marketing.
(Emphasis on '*Strategic*'.)

~~~~~~~~~~~

You should avoid
Using mobile devices,
Including laptops,
With a public, Wi-Fi connection.

~~~~~~~~~~~

The same word
Can have different meanings
To different people.
So be aware of how you say,
What you say.

~~~~~~~~~~~

Humor is a great ice-breaker.

Seek out awards.
Even if you don't win,
You will still gain much exposure.

~~~~~~~~~

The more staff that you employ
Who are simply there for a paycheck,
The less likely that your business
Is reaching it's profit
And growth potential.
You also need staff
That gets excited from seeing
The business grow,
Knowing that they helped
It happen.

~~~~~~~~~

Unresolved conflicts
Will eventually boil over
And '*burn*' someone.

Are employees paying attention
To what is being said,
Or are they faking it?
Know how to spot the difference.

~~~~~~~~~~

Solicit meeting agenda topics
From those who will not be attending,
As well as from planned participants.
You will be surprised by
The value in doing this.

~~~~~~~~~~

Have detailed, written
Job descriptions
For all employees,
Including management.

~~~~~~~~~~

Understand
That '*non-compete*' agreements
Are often non-enforceable.

~~~~~~~~~

Yes,
You *can* transfer staff
To another location.
But if they do not
Want the move,
What makes you think
That they will not '*jump ship*'?

~~~~~~~~~

It's been said many times,
But it bears repeating:
Entrepreneurs have exchanged
One boss over them
For countless others.

Arguing
With staff or bosses
Will cost you dearly,
In most instances.

~~~~~~~~~~

You don't always need
To print in color.
Think of how small costs
Add up.

~~~~~~~~~~

Remembering lessons
Learned from past experiences
Is not the same as
Dwelling on and rehashing
Failures over and over, again.

~~~~~~~~~~

Remaining '*flexible*'
Does not preclude you
From holding firm
To your core beliefs.

~~~~~~~~

'*Slip and fall*' accidents
Are a leading cause of lawsuits.
Ensure that your premises
Are clear of potential obstacles,
Spills, and other dangers.

~~~~~~~~~

When was the last time
That you had
Fire extinguishers and alarms
Tested/replaced?

~~~~~~~~

While holiday parties
Can be great for morale,
Employees might want or need
A bonus check, more.

~~~~~~~~~~

Plan time limits for meetings,
But only as a guideline.
Some discussions need to lead to
Action/plans before adjournment.

~~~~~~~~~~

Time
Is not your enemy.
Mis-management of it,
However, is.

~~~~~~~~~~

Do you dress for success?

When you ask for advice,
You are not obligated to follow it.
But, you are obligated
To be respectful to the one giving it.

~~~~~~~~~

Pay attention to shifts in power.

~~~~~~~~~

Know when to look
For another job.
Know when to turn down
A promotion.

~~~~~~~~~

Keep an eye out
For teachable moments.

~~~~~~~~~

Being '*the boss's pet*'
Comes with restrictions
And liabilities of it's own.
Do you really wish to be
Somebody's '*lapdog*'?

~~~~~~~~~~

Express messages of
Congratulations or condolences
In person.
If not possible,
Then use a physical card
And not an email.

~~~~~~~~~~

Be careful
When comparing the total sales
Of full and part-time employees.
Do they have equal opportunities
To close sales?

Maintain proper insurance,
At all times.
Health. Property.
Cyber-security.
Fire. Theft. Flood.
Life. Accident.
Workers' compensation.
And whatever others that
Your insurance agent, lawyer,
And government suggests/requires.

~~~~~~~~~~

Your personal life
Is important
To you.
But, probably of
Little consequence
To your boss or clients.
So don't bore them with
Your life's many details.

No sale is too small.
However, some sales
Are too big.
You could never
Properly fulfill the order.
So pass it up.

~~~~~~~~~~

Great salespeople,
Work harder
When they are not
On a fixed salary,
But, rather on commission.
(Or, commission plus a base pay.)

~~~~~~~~~~

Consultants
Are not 'miracle workers'.
So, do not expect
Unrealistic results.

'Turning the other cheek' works
As long as you are prepared
For the possibility of
Having the other one slapped.

~~~~~~~~~~

Accept
Well-intentioned criticism,
Graciously.
For there is *always*
Room for improvement.

~~~~~~~~~~

Avoid *'charged'* topics
Of conversation,
Regardless of
How tempting they are.

~~~~~~~~~~

When resolving employee conflicts,
Bear in mind that everyone involved
Will remember the specifics
Of the situation, differently.
Believing that *their* version
Is the only accurate one.

~~~~~~~~~~~

Do not bluff or lie.
No matter how tempting
Or convenient that it might be.
It *will* come back to '*bite*' you.
Usually, when you least expect it.
And, when you can least afford it to.

~~~~~~~~~~~

Badmouthing your company
In front of *or* directly to clients
Is unacceptable.

Perception.
Perception.
Perception.
Know that it is often
Your client or staff's '*reality*'.

~~~~~~~~~~

Companies,
That '*throw away*' employees
As if they were disposable pens,
Seldom attract or keep
Qualified and loyal staff.

~~~~~~~~~~

You can be known for
Caring about employees' families
Without being
Intimately involved with them.

~~~~~~~~~~

Great ideas can have
High upfront $$$ costs,
Yet produce high value results.
So, don't dismiss them, out of hand.

~~~~~~~~~~

Not all advertising works.
Learn how to evaluate results.
Or hire someone who does know.
(The latter is worth the investment.)

~~~~~~~~~~

Yes, repairs can be costly.
But, putting them off
Typically results in
Even more costly ones.
(Sort of like not facing *any* problem.)

~~~~~~~~~~

Set a goal for
'*X*' number of failures.
Why?
Because doing so will help you
To accept them better,
When they occur.
And, failures *will* happen,
Along with successes.

~~~~~~~~~~

When training staff,
Be cognizant of
Their potential and
Their current capabilities.

~~~~~~~~~~

Do not make donating
To charitable contributions
Mandatory.

Different cultures.
They impact your business
And your job
In multiple ways.
So make the most of
'*The opportunity*'!

~~~~~~~~~~

Threatening terms and tones
Don't instill a sense of loyalty,
Or inspire staff to greatness.
So, choose your words and tones,
Carefully.

~~~~~~~~~~

Leaving one's problems
At the door of the business
Is often unrealistic.
So don't expect it.
Be grateful if it does occur.

Because people work all hours,
Wanting products and services
When *they* decide they need them,
Consider having flexible hours.

~~~~~~~~

In the event of
A partner divorce or death,
The company needs
Established procedures
Plus a business continuity plan.
This way, the company can continue
With as little interruption
And turmoil as possible.

~~~~~~~~

Remain current on changes
And trends in your profession.
Utilize podcasts, news aggregators,
And independent researchers.

When was the last time
That you delegated?
That is a crucial management
Responsibility.

~~~~~~~~~~

Dishonest employees,
Customers, suppliers...
Are to be expected and planned for.
(Shrinkage, embezzlement,...)

~~~~~~~~~~

An investment in
A video surveillance system
Can be a great deterrence to theft
As well as a way to review
Foot traffic and other customer
Patterns, during the day's course.

~~~~~~~~~~

Stay on top of energy usage.
Have a yearly energy audit.

~~~~~~~~~

The myth of a manager or owner
Being capable of '*running the show*',
Single-handedly,
Is simply that: *A myth*.
No one can do it all *or* do it all, well.

~~~~~~~~~

Trust your staff
To do their job.
Or, train them better.
Or, hire new staff.
But be confident that
They can perform
To '*the standards*' that you set.

~~~~~~~~~

Keep an updated resume,
On hand.
You never know
When you might want it.

~~~~~~~~~~~~

Offer carpooling, gas cards,
Or other transportation aid,
Whenever possible.

~~~~~~~~~~~~

Attend public hearings
That could impact your company
For the better or the worse.

~~~~~~~~~~~~

Minimize
Inventory on-hand
In order to maximize profits.

Consider being a
Fragrance-free office/workplace
As there are many asthmatics
Who *do* try to avoid doing business
With companies who are not.

~~~~~~~~~

Keep children's books on-hand
In waiting rooms.
It's a small gesture that
Can result in a huge pay-off.

~~~~~~~~~

Airing politically-charged shows
In your waiting room
Will likely get your clients/patients
Agitated.
Not a state-of-mind that you relish.

~~~~~~~~~

If you are willing
To risk your own finances
And homes,
Then investors will consider
Helping you out.
Otherwise, why should they?

~~~~~~~~~

Retailers
Who constantly have
'Help Wanted' signs in their windows
Are signaling that they are not
The place for longterm employment.
Is that the message that you
Truly wish to broadcast?

~~~~~~~~~

Learn how to use social media,
Even if you will delegate the task
To someone else, on a daily basis.

Hire a risk manager, yearly,
To evaluate the business property
And work-flow procedures.

~~~~~~~~~

It might not be fair,
But you *will* be judged
By the company that you keep.

~~~~~~~~~

Discrimination can rear it's ugly head
In the unlikeliest of situations.
Do not tolerate it.
Period.
Exclamation mark!

~~~~~~~~~

Even great consultants
Will not hit home runs, every time.

Have clear, disseminated,
'*Lawyer-approved*' policies covering
Sexual harassment, bullying,
Workplace violence, hazing,
Theft, and falsifying of records.
Because one or more of these
Will arise, eventually.

~~~~~~~~~~

Yes,
Money is not '*the only motivator*'.
But, for most it is a primary one.
So, pay employees well
And positive results
Become a more likely outcome.
Thereby increasing your
Bottom-line profits.

~~~~~~~~~~

Always be prepared for a tax audit.

Allowing insubordination
To go unchecked,
Can lead to mass disrespect,
A breakdown in productivity,
And a loss of customer satisfaction.

~~~~~~~~~

Neither '*wimps*'
Nor '*tyrants*'
Make for great
Company presidents.

~~~~~~~~~

Unannounced site visits
Can reveal much.
Good and bad.
Yet, what you should know.

~~~~~~~~~

Equipment breaks down,
Key employees become ill,
Orders get mixed-up.
For these and other
'Murphy's Law' situations,
Always (!) have a backup plan.

~~~~~~~~~

As with your personal finances,
Have an *'emergency fund'* set aside
For your company's needs.

~~~~~~~~~

Sometimes we are unaware
That we are being rude,
Disrespectful, or arrogant.
It is your staff's obligation
To inform us of it,
In a positive,
Yet direct manner.

Food cost will make
Or break a restaurant.
And it's importance is often
Ignored or underestimated.

~~~~~~~~~

One method for reducing
Fighting among salespeople
Is to give them all
A much higher hourly pay
And eliminate commissions.
(*A side benefit of this policy:*
Customers feel less pressured,
More relaxed, and will spend $$.)

~~~~~~~~~

Offer your employees
Discounts that are greater
Than what you give
To your customers.

If a location has been home
To multiple businesses
During a short time period,
Think long and hard
As to why you believe
That *you* will succeed there,
When others have not.
(*Especially if these were similar*
businesses to yours.)

~~~~~~~~~

Have clear, well-defined,
And visible return policies.

~~~~~~~~~

Know when it is appropriate
To flaunt your wealth and success.
(*It could be the correct move to make.*)

~~~~~~~~~

Every business needs
A well-designed website.
That is kept up-to-date.

~~~~~~~~~

Observe
What successful competitors
Are doing
And imitate what could work
In your own business.

~~~~~~~~~

Staff are constantly '*trained*'
By observing your actions,
Whether or not you realize it.

~~~~~~~~~

Don't expect loyalty from staff
If you do not exhibit loyalty to them.

Allow for employees
To telecommute,
Where appropriate,
And with technology safeguards
In place.

~~~~~~~~~~

Don't skimp
On paying for staff
Who have real expertise
In their field.

~~~~~~~~~~

When buying '*Local*',
Don't overlook
Your satellite locations.

~~~~~~~~~~

Give credit where it is due.

**Ambition
Is a double-edged sword.
Do not allow it
To consume you.**

~~~~~~~~~

**Zero-tolerance policies
Are usually less fair
And more problematic
Than those that require thought,
Planning, and a willingness
To deal with matters on their merit.**

~~~~~~~~~

Think carefully.
**Is there value in correcting
Every mistake that staff makes?**

~~~~~~~~~

Everyone craves praise
For a job well-done.
Don't skimp on dishing it out.

~~~~~~~~~~

Do not tolerate illegal behavior
Caused by top management
Or, the owners.

~~~~~~~~~~

Learn the art of '*CYA*'
('*Cover Your Ass*').

~~~~~~~~~~

Know the legal ramifications
Of providing or allowing liquor
On your premises
Or at a company event, elsewhere.
Hint: *They can be devastating.*

There will always be those
Who admire *'glitz'*
And those who admire
The *'modest'* and the *'sedate'*.
So, just be yourself.
Well-earned praise *will* find you.

~~~~~~~~~~

You might have the skills
But lack *'the stomach'*
For owning your own business.
There is no shame in that.
None at all.

~~~~~~~~~~

Every job
Is important.
Every job.

~~~~~~~~~~

Hiring someone
Is always a gamble.
Don't let that stop you
From hiring needed assistance.

~~~~~~~~~~

Poll your customers
Regarding ways
That you can
Improve your service.

~~~~~~~~~~

Want to increase foot traffic?
Offer free, inexpensive food.
It works (*almost*) every time!

~~~~~~~~~~

Don't ramble.

Avoid overdosing on meetings.

~~~~~~~~~

**Every employee and customer
Is capable of making
Positive contributions
Toward your career
And the company's bottom-line.
Help to draw those out of them.**

~~~~~~~~~

**Avoid using technology
For it's own sake
Or to appear '*hip*'.**

~~~~~~~~~

**Sometimes you need to
'*Bite the bullet*',
When seeking alternative financing.**

Although asking someone
To '*keep it secret*'
Is often the fastest way
To get a message out among staff,
It is not the preferred way,
As it usually becomes distorted,
When it is re-told and re-told and…

~~~~~~~~~~

Please don't be offended by this:
But you are not a teen, anymore.
Everything does not revolve
Around you and your wants.

~~~~~~~~~~

Do not oversell.
Customers will find out
And will rebel.

~~~~~~~~~~

Remember to
Patent, trademark, or copyright
Your works.
For great ideas will be copied.
(At least, someone will try to do so.
And lawsuits can be quite messy
And expensive.)

~~~~~~~~~~

Once you settle
A bogus claim against you,
The more such claims will appear.

~~~~~~~~~~

Remember that unfortunately,
Not all *angel investors*
Have *pure intentions*.
Be vigilant when dealing with them.

~~~~~~~~~~

Customers seldom trust
'Going Out Of Business' sales.

~~~~~~~~~~

Do not create ads
That are so clever or enjoyable
That viewers do not remember
The name of the product or business.

~~~~~~~~~~

When it comes to legal matters
Get professional advice.
And, while they might charge
A small fortune per hour,
Rest assured that lawyers are
Probably less costly than
Facing litigation, down the road.

~~~~~~~~~~

Be prepared to answer questions
From potential clients.
And, if you do not know
The information that is sought,
Never bluff or lie.

~~~~~~~~~~

Employees are fearful of mergers.
Assuage their concerns,
If you can.
But, always be honest with them.

~~~~~~~~~~

When hiring:
Neither the most educated
Nor the most experienced applicant
Should *automatically*
Be offered the position.

~~~~~~~~~~

Fiscal responsibility
Can free you from (some) worries,
So that you can better focus
On making your venture
More profitable.

~~~~~~~~~

Avoid antagonizing bankers
Or other investors,
Unless you can afford
To walk away from them
And their dollars.

~~~~~~~~~

Indulge in more fun
And with less potential liabilities
By not having booze at office parties.

~~~~~~~~~

Have you thought
About what you would do
If you were ever laid-off,
Fired, or lost the business?
You need to,
Because '*Life happens*'.
Be prepared.

~~~~~~~~~~

Job hunting?
Don't assume
That the interviewer knows
What is truly important to you
In terms of working conditions,
Perks, salary, and duties.
It is up to you
To let them know.

~~~~~~~~~~

Learn proper dining etiquette.

Reputations
Are extremely difficult
To change.

~~~~~~~~~

Creative thinkers and inventors
Pay the '*wheel*'
(that they are not re-inventing)
It's due.

~~~~~~~~~

Flirting
Might seem to make
The workplace more fun,
But it is skirting and flirting
With a lawsuit or worse.

~~~~~~~~~

Make use of mystery shoppers.

'*Protecting*' your ideas
By not working
Toward their implementation,
Will lead to regrets
And the likelihood that
Someone else will come forward
And get the rewards,
Instead of you.

~~~~~~~~~~

If you are seen as a '*bully*'
Or a '*know-it-all*',
Folks will seldom take your side,
Even when they should do so.

~~~~~~~~~~

Consider the lead of governments
And your competitors:
Utilize *Open Source* software.

All employees should know
The company's policies
Regarding robberies, threats,
Shooters, inclement weather,
Natural disasters…

~~~~~~~~~~

Off-shoring customer service
Might save you dollars, upfront.
However, it will likely
Cost you more money
In the long-run.

~~~~~~~~~~

Don't give employees
Corporate credit cards
With unnecessary spending limits.

~~~~~~~~~~

Although you are the business owner,
You are not automatically entitled
To take a vacation or receive
A raise in pay.
You need to earn it,
And, as importantly,
Be able to afford it.

~~~~~~~~~~~

Don't share or house
Your client database
Without written guarantees
That the company will not share
Your info with competitors.

~~~~~~~~~~~

Have clear and consistent
Business hours
For both the public and employees.

**Be polite and professional
To customers, employees,
Bankers and suppliers.**
Heck, to anyone!

~~~~~~~~~~~

**Great ideas
Require great timing
To be successful.
Is '*now*' the right time?**

~~~~~~~~~~~

**Remember:
Planning.
Planning.
Planning.**

~~~~~~~~~~~

Maintain great customer records.

When conducting a training session,
Do not read word-for-word
From a manual,
Unless you are quoting
A law or something akin to that.

~~~~~~~~~~

Make yourself
More valuable to employers.
Learn others' jobs or new skills,
If you can.

~~~~~~~~~~

Avoid wasting time
Trying to game the system.

~~~~~~~~~~

Don't pour out your heart
On social media.

Observe and analyze
A potential client
Before you meet with them.
(Their dress, demeanor...
Can all give you clues
As to how best to approach
This specific individual.)

~~~~~~~~

Don't overlook
The potential goodwill
That sponsoring
A school athletic team,
Section of a highway,
Or other program,
Can provide you.

~~~~~~~~

Cross-train staff.

Reward Programs for clients
Who refer others to your business
Can backfire, if they feel
Too pressured to join the program.

~~~~~~~~~

Are you proud
Of the things that you do
To get ahead?

~~~~~~~~~

Have job descriptions available
For people to read
In advance of applying
For a position.

~~~~~~~~~

Avoid making yourself feel superior
By degrading employees.

Before you move near
A major competitor
Learn whether or not
They are making a profit.
Or, if there is even a market
For your products/services, there.

~~~~~~~~~~

Leading by example,
Is critical to success.

~~~~~~~~~~

Would hiring additional staff
Boost your bottom-line, sufficiently?
If the answer is '*Yes*',
Then what are you waiting for?

~~~~~~~~~~

Read biographies of role models.

Recharging your batteries
Is not an option
If you long for
Long-term success.

~~~~~~~~~~

Most scandals are avoidable.
Yet, others are inevitable.
So, expect them.
Prepare as much as possible for them.

~~~~~~~~~~

Be proud of your successes.
Don't brag about them.

~~~~~~~~~~

A lie by omission
Is still a lie.
Partners will never forget it.

Don't waste time and money,
Assuming that all staff
Needs identical training,
Based solely upon
The title of their position.

~~~~~~~~~~

Although it is natural
To have '*Favorites*',
Try to not let it show,
As that will lead to
Jealousy among the others.

~~~~~~~~~~

'*Sexy*'
Is appealing.
'*Sexism*'
Is quite the opposite.

~~~~~~~~~~

Seldom should you
Terminate an employee
Without first waiting a day,
In order to further evaluate
Your decision...
Making certain
That it is not based
Solely, or even largely,
On emotions.

~~~~~~~~~

When was the last time
That you verbally
Patted a co-worker
On the back
For a job well-done?

~~~~~~~~~

Keep physically fit,
So that you remain mentally alert.

Just as every employee
Is expendable,
So is every employer.
Work to keep valuable staff.

~~~~~~~~~~

Hitching your professional life
To a politician
Can easily derail
Your career and business.
Tread carefully.

~~~~~~~~~~

Sharing too much
Personal information
Is dangerous.
In many ways.
Use discretion.
For today's friend
Might become tomorrow's foe.

**Don't over-analyze.
Don't over-plan.
Don't wait too long.**

~~~~~~~~~

**Neither '*Always Open*'
Nor '*Always Closed*'
Door policies
Should be acceptable.**

~~~~~~~~~

**Bankers see past scapegoats
When you seek extensions
On loan due dates
Or, even request new loans.**

~~~~~~~~~

**Ask employees for feedback
Regarding their supervisor/s.**

The more that
You stress your '*honesty*',
The less that customers
Will believe it.

~~~~~~~~~~~

The most efficient method
Is not always
The quickest one
To implement.

~~~~~~~~~~~

Things will not always go your way.
But, that shouldn't do more than
'*Slow you down*',
Temporarily.

~~~~~~~~~~~

Make time for family and friends.

Technology should be implemented,
Judiciously.

~~~~~~~~~

Set specific, detailed goals,
As opposed to vague ones.

~~~~~~~~~

Sometimes, great ideas
Come from those
Who do not even work
In that department.

~~~~~~~~~

Hope for loyalty from staff
But do not count on it.

~~~~~~~~~

Use a '*Responsive*'-designed website,
If you can.

~~~~~~~~~

Some topics
Should not be discussed
During a meeting.
A phone call, fax, email, or text
Might serve all involved, better.

~~~~~~~~~

Simply because you *can* star
In your own commercial,
Does not mean that you should do so.

~~~~~~~~~

Practice.
Leads to proficiency.
That simple.

Try not to overstay your welcome.
Know when it is time to move on.
And, upward.

~~~~~~~~~~~

Pitting employees
Against one another,
Rarely works out,
In the long or short run.

~~~~~~~~~~~

Court the media.
But realize that if a '*negative*' story
Comes their way as a result of it,
'*All bets are off*'.

~~~~~~~~~~~

Keep personnel records
In a secure location.

Management styles
Should take
Your current workforce
Into consideration.

~~~~~~~~~

You will never be able
To fully anticipate
All problems.
So don't worry about the ones
Which you could not plan for.
Simply do your best.

~~~~~~~~~

Provide your staff
Who attend conferences
With a realistic spending allowance,
Taking the location into account.

~~~~~~~~~

Examine unrelated industries
For ideas that could be adapted
To your world.

~~~~~~~~~

Attempt to make meetings
'Interesting',
Rather than *'fun'*.

~~~~~~~~~

Have a formal chain of command
That everyone knows.

~~~~~~~~~

'Talent'
Is in the eyes of the beholder.
So, check references
From multiple sources,
Before hiring someone.

If many customers
Voice the same complaint,
Then consider that it is either
A legitimate one
Or a perceived one.
Either way, take action.

~~~~~~~~~~

People want a '*bargain*'.
Even if they suspect that
It is only an artificial one.

~~~~~~~~~~

Be creative
For those times
When you cannot afford
To give employees
A cash raise.

~~~~~~~~~~

When emailing
Current and prospective clients,
Offer some valuable content
For their use,
In addition to your sales pitch.

~~~~~~~~~

Don't count on
Your company's pension.
Contracts change
Or otherwise get broken.

~~~~~~~~~

Think of a lawyer
Who is on retainer
As simply
Another form of insurance.

~~~~~~~~~

Navigating the waters of
'Political correctness'
Is extremely difficult.
Why?
Because you are likely
To insult someone
Regardless
Of what you say or do.

~~~~~~~~~

Your employees
Might not vocalize
Their displeasure
With your policies.
But they will display it
In other, non-productive ways.
So, encourage honest feedback.

~~~~~~~~~

Don't ignore complaints.

'Exit strategies'
Need attention to detail
As though they were *'Entrance'* ones.

~~~~~~~~~~

No tweet, email, or social media post
Can properly convey
Your attitude or tone.
(Not even *'LOL'*'s, smiley faces, or...)
Face-to-face contact still rocks!

~~~~~~~~~~

Being skilled in your *'craft'*
Is usually not the same skill set
As what management
Or ownership positions
Require in order to breed success.

~~~~~~~~~~

Learn about
A company's reference policy
Before trusting
A prospective employee's reference.
Does everyone get a great/poor one?

~~~~~~~~~

Yes,
Every employee *is* dispensable.
However, can you get by
While a replacement
Is hired, trained,
And becomes acclimated
To your company?

~~~~~~~~~

Depending upon
A manager's leadership style,
It is not worth attempting
To implement some strategies.

Business plans
Must be '*living documents*'.
Subject to frequent
Review and evaluation.
Changes, as called for.

~~~~~~~~~~

Always respond promptly
To a message left for you.
Who knows
When you might need them
To respond quickly to you?

~~~~~~~~~~

If you have a reputation for
Arrogance, exaggeration,
Or bad-mouthing competitors,
You will lose business.
So, earn a 'solid' reputation.

~~~~~~~~~~

Not everyone
Is cut out to tape
Their own commercials.
Consider hiring even
'*B*' list, well-known actors
Or local radio/TV talent, instead.

~~~~~~~~~~~

Delegate.
Delegate.
Delegate.
Or,
Fail.
Fail.
Fail.

~~~~~~~~~~~

Think as a client would think.

~~~~~~~~~~~

Keep handy:
Free mobile apps to help with
First aid, natural disasters,
Emergencies,
And vehicular accidents.

~~~~~~~~~

Consider being open for business,
During some of the hours
When your competitors are not.

~~~~~~~~~

Ask who specifically has the authority
To resolve your issue,
Because your assumption
Might be inaccurate.

~~~~~~~~~

The best clients recognize skill.

The root causes of problems
Are often hidden from view.
Take time to learn unearth them.

~~~~~~~~~~

Do not discipline staff
In front of or within earshot of
Other employees or customers.
You will appear '*mean*' or '*uncaring*'.

~~~~~~~~~~

New methods which are
Thought by staff
To be '*inconvenient*'
Or '*unworkable*'
Often prove to be otherwise,
Once they become fluent
In utilizing them.

~~~~~~~~~~

Closed door meetings,
Especially when your business
Is doing poorly,
Breeds gossip and concerns
Regarding job security.
So, use them judiciously.

~~~~~~~~~~

Consider the benefits
Of allowing staff to telework:
During storms,
During an epidemic,
When their children are ill,
Simply because they want to do so...

~~~~~~~~~~

Managers should not supervise
Immediate family members
Or romantic interests.

Mine historical data.
(*i.e.*, Which day of the week is busiest,
Has the highest sales volume,
And results in the most profit.)

~~~~~~~~~~~

Know who to call when
A scandal breaks,
Or when it is developing.

~~~~~~~~~~~

Have a formal
Inclement weather policy.

~~~~~~~~~~~

Good employees
Desire feedback.
Poorly performing ones
Fear it.

Occasionally,
Actions or reactions
Are neither *'right'* nor *'wrong'*.
They simply *'are'*.

~~~~~~~~~~~~~~~

Avoid
Reinventing the wheel.

~~~~~~~~~~~~~~~

Embrace LEAN techniques.
Shed excess processes.

~~~~~~~~~~~~~~~

What appears on the web,
Including social media,
Remains somewhere on the web
***'Forever'*.**

The more that you treat employees
With respect & appropriate benefits,
The less likely it is
That they will turn to unions
Or go out on strikes.

~~~~~~~~~~

Pay attention to how
Customers and employees
React to you.
Learn from this
Valuable information.
(*Regardless of whether or not
You agree with their assessment.*)

~~~~~~~~~~

More experience on the job
Does not automatically
Equate to a higher skill level.

Do nice things for someone
Before you need or want
To request a favor from them.

~~~~~~~~~

Do not dismiss suggestions
From anyone,
Out-of-hand.
Or, you might be dismissing
A '*winning idea*'.

~~~~~~~~~

Be careful.
You will seldom know
Who is related to/or otherwise knows
People whom you are bad-mouthing.

~~~~~~~~~

Improve your vocabulary.

Simply because a company is huge
Or an industry leader,
Does not mean that
Their marketing strategies
Are truly effective
Or would apply to your business.

~~~~~~~~~

You will not always be
The '*smartest person in the room*'.
But, don't get hung-up on that fact.

~~~~~~~~~

Beware of treating some clients
Better than others.
If word gets out about this practice,
You could lose
Many of the '*non-favored*' ones.

~~~~~~~~~

Do you know
What your employee
Is dealing with at home?
Home-life *does* impact work-life.

~~~~~~~~~~

Develop a plan for the
Continuity of ownership,
Upon any possible crisis occurring.

~~~~~~~~~~

Employee evaluations
Should be fair and unbiased.
Yet, still, judgmental.

~~~~~~~~~~

Learn how to
Properly use
Social media.

Don't be afraid of refusing
A customer's requests/demands.
But, then respond back to them
With a counter-offer.

~~~~~~~~~~

Never allow yourself
To get into a screaming match
With an employee.
Even if you both
Are behind closed doors.

~~~~~~~~~~

Register website domains
That include variations of
Your company and personal name.

~~~~~~~~~~

Compromising is a key to success.

Monitor review sites.
Respond quickly
To any negative reviews.
Be *'classy'*, not *'defensive'*/*'offensive'*.

~~~~~~~~~~

Occasionally,
Suspend your belief.

~~~~~~~~~~

Know when it is time
To close your business
And begin a *'new chapter'*
In your life.

~~~~~~~~~~

Never feel ashamed
For trying to live *'Your Dream'*
If you go bankrupt.

The '*look*' and layout
Of your company
Plays a crucial role
In your business's
Success or lack thereof.

~~~~~~~~~~~

Printing pages, duplex,
Can save money.

~~~~~~~~~~~

Remember that
What you say in confidence
Always has the potential
To be shared with others.
Always.

~~~~~~~~~~~

Change locks, periodically.

Reward suggestions
That you choose to implement,
Regardless of
Their ultimate success or failure.

~~~~~~~~~

Neither employees nor employers
Should Tweet, check Facebook,
Or read their personal emails,
When they are '*on the clock*',
Unless it is required or approved of.

~~~~~~~~~

Be sensitive to
Language differences.
Especially colloquialisms.

~~~~~~~~~

We often misread body language.

Get to know the local,
National, and business beat reporters.

~~~~~~~~~~

Do you actually
Listen to your staff?
Or, only appear to do so?
They need to know that
They can *really* have
Your undivided attention.

~~~~~~~~~~

Customers are not always correct.
Plan how you and your staff
Will respond when they are 'off-base',
Or simply obnoxious.

~~~~~~~~~~

Many worthwhile results
Require a lengthy process.

~~~~~~~~~~~~

Some battles
Are not worth fighting.
Choose the ones
That you engage in
Carefully.

~~~~~~~~~~~~

When you go to '*war*'
Be certain to know your '*enemy's*'
Strengths as well as weaknesses.

~~~~~~~~~~~~

Know when to retreat
In order to
Fight another day.

Engaging in nepotism
Might be '*your right*'.
However, it usually
Leads to serious
Morale issues.

~~~~~~~~~~

You do not
Have to like someone
In order to trust them.

~~~~~~~~~~

Always, always
Have a lawyer
Review a contract
Before you sign it.

~~~~~~~~~~

Register a domain in your name.

If your company has a reputation
For treating clients and staff, well,
You will seldom be at a loss for either.

~~~~~~~~~~

Sometimes, you need to
Back your employees,
Instead of your customers.

~~~~~~~~~~

Every '*Boss*' reports to '*Someone*'.

~~~~~~~~~~

Don't over-think matters.

~~~~~~~~~~

We all have '*erasers on our pencils*'.
Don't afraid to use them.

Continuous improvement
Is more than simply
Revamping a process, once.
It is a commitment
That should lead to
Increased profits and satisfaction
By both staff and customers.

~~~~~~~~~

Your physical and mental health
Impacts your job performance,
As well as your job satisfaction.

~~~~~~~~~

Support your staff
When they deserve it.
Even at a customer's expense.

~~~~~~~~~

Raise the bar:
**Make your company
The one that everyone
Wishes to work for.**

~~~~~~~~~

**Although some problems
Will go away without
You taking any overt action,
The overwhelming majority will
Require some level of your attention.**

~~~~~~~~~

Don't be afraid to manage.

~~~~~~~~~

**Remember
That your business account
Is not your personal '*piggy bank*'.**

There will always be someone who is:
Smarter. Smoother.
More attractive. More attentive.
Friendlier. More personable.
More loyal. More trustworthy.
More...
And, so what?
Simply be the best that you can be!
(And keep working on
Continuous improvements...)

~~~~~~~~~~

Control your social media presence.

~~~~~~~~~~

Most employees could/should
Be successfully cross-trained.
For everyone's benefit.

~~~~~~~~~~

You will always
Leave a conference or meeting
With new information/insight.
Sometimes a little.
Sometimes a lot.

~~~~~~~~~~

Compromise is a key component
Of successful negotiations.

~~~~~~~~~~

Believe in yourself.
Believe in your employees.
Value your clients.

~~~~~~~~~~

And, lead your company and life
So that when you die
You will be mourned and missed.

Succeed!

CONCLUSION

Thank you for making an investment in your future.

The fact of the matter is that we tend to overlook the incredible value that lies in '*stepping back*' a bit from our current situations and examining what is '*The Obvious*'.

You only need to think of co-workers, bosses, or other business owners who experienced mis-steps, whether '*major ones*' or only '*hiccups*', to eventually recognize what they *should have* done. Help avoid making many of these mistakes, by reading the advice contained here in *Maximize Your Business Success - Don't Overlook The Obvious*.

Keep this book handy. Because what applies to your current situation, today, might no longer work for you, tomorrow or next month. And, something which appeared to be irrelevant, in the here-and-now, could suddenly result in an '*Aha!*' moment for you, very soon!

A huge part of '*success*' comes from sharing tips with others. From helping them to achieve. In that way, you make life better for all of us.
So it is that I hope you will recommend this book to those whom you respect and care about.

Please send me an email to share your success stories. You can contact me at: Russ@MaximizeYourBusinessSuccess.com

Now, go and make the best of your life, personally and professionally! - 'Nuff said.

Russ